Turtle Blessing

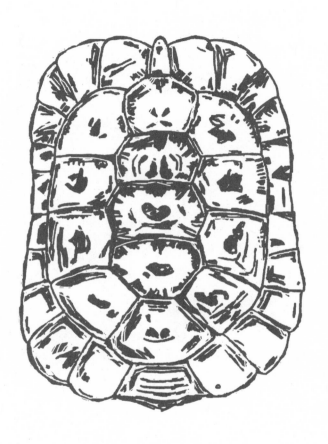

TURTLE
BLESSING

Penny Harter

La Alameda Press • New Mexico

For Bill

The following poems appear in the indicated publications:

"Deer Crossing", Honorable Mention, National Poetry Competition, 1988, sponsored by the Chester H. Jones Foundation; "Just There", "Light Years", "Willow", "For a Great Horned Owl", and "Asleep, You are a River", *The Christian Science Monitor;* "Whale Song," in *The Dolphin's Arc* (SCOP Publications, Inc.); "The Way Home", *Edge* (Tokyo); "Tulip", *5 am.;* "The Llano" *Gaia* (Whistle Press, Inc.); "Frogs in the Rice Paddy, Kawasaki", *Karamu;* "Dream Time", in *World's Edge* (Word Press, Japan/Open Meeting Books, Kenosha) & in *Life on the Line* (Negative Capability Press); "Vision Quest", in *A Nation Within, Contemporary Native American Writing* (Outrigger Publishers, New Zealand); "Reading the Tea Leaves", won the Mary Carolyn Davies Memorial Award from the Poetry Society of America; published in *Parallels: Artists & Poets* (Midmarch Arts Press); "A Circle of Sheep", *Phoenix;* "The Sun on Sandia Crest", in *Saludos! Poems of New Mexico* (Pennywhistle Press); "The Only Cows Left in Piscataway", "Living on a County Highway", and "Sister Death", in *The Price of Admission* (From Here Press); "How Can We Not?", *Sing Heavenly Muse!;* "Living On a County Highway", *Spectrum;* "Turtle Blessing", *Stockpot;* "Turtle Blessing", "Sister Death", and "Tulip" in *Two Worlds Walking* (New Rivers Press).

ISBN :: 1-888809-01-9
Library of Congress No. :: 96-84345

La Alameda Press
9636 Guadalupe Trail NW
Albuquerque, New Mexico 87114

CONTENTS

Dream Time

*In Australia the totemic ancestors walked across the land
leaving words and musical notes in their footprints.
The aboriginals read the country as a musical score.*

In the Dream Time,
the Ancestors went underground,
Honey-Ant here, Wallaby there,
after their magic feet
had planted songs in the dust,

and by these songs, the people
learned each totem path,
singing the holy hillock, sacred spring,
and burning bush of their clan;
mapping kinship where the tongue shifted
but the song continued,
humming up from the underworld
like the first rivers.

When I listen to the whales
calling deep sea currents alive,
their repeating melodies answered
across great distances;
when I hear the wolves, the birds—
all the tribes descended from the Ancestors
learning the planet by ear,
defining it by song

as the wind does each tree,
I do what I can,
throwing this song out from my house
like a rope in search of water
through the fire.

The Llano

Stark as piñon
cows graze the horizon,
adrift in a field of light.

Around them, mountains
hold sky on dark flanks,
ancient muscles rippling
under the sun.

Above the cows a storm gathers,
herding lightning around the pasture
purple as twilight.

As the Earth tilts toward night,
the hills turn to blood,
and we come home,
kicking the dust of the road
into starlight.

Buffalo

Heavy as petrified wood,
you stare from the rock face,
slow body aging in the moonlight,
feet lost in crevices.

You sniff the air.
It is not the same wind
you remember.
Your mouth is as cold
as the sky.

Frame Drum

Often I think of sitting cross-legged,
knees supple as a child's.
I bow to touch my forehead to the dirt,
make a sacred hoop of my bare arms,
and lay it gently on the quiet earth.
Then I draw the circle, drum it
with my palms until the frame quivers,
until the sky goes dark with birds,
the ground with hooves,
all the way in.

The Sun on Sandia Crest

On Sandia Crest, the sun
stuns the Earth,
its huge blinding eye
turning snow to fire.

It swells in the absolute
blue of the sky,
its dark pupil fueling
luminous, uneven lunges
of the corona.

Or it is a mouth
with many tongues
licking up the mountains,
the slopes of blue spruce.

It swallows the radio towers,
inhales the lookout platform.

This sun finds the bones
beneath our cheeks, the small
white echoes of our skulls
which will not shine
unless they are an offering
scattered on the mountainside.

Heading West

An avenue of stones stretches behind me,
rough faces searching the sky.

A river of bees follows in my wake
humming a former century.

Signpost after signpost is wrapped in rags,
swaying in the wind that blows steadily
at my back.

For some time now
I have been dropping things
along the way, though the memory
of what I leave behind clings
to my ankles like a beggar.

Much farther back
are the things I let go.
Orphans by the roadside,
they no longer call me from my life.

Ahead of me, the mountains beckon,
dividing night from day,
and all roads seem to rise
into their snow.

Dusk at White Rock Overlook

Cumulus rise from the ridges.
The river glints brown in the gorge.
Thunderheads deepen the mountains.
Soon it will be evening.

Two ravens float from the cliff edge.
Their shadows follow the current.
Long ripples drift in the canyon
Carrying darkness to shore.

This is the clock of the shadow.
This is the gong of the skin.
Rock walls spill down to the water
Taking what's left of the sun.

Solar Eclipse, New Mexico

The great rim of the sun
grazes on red cliffs
as it rises to meet
this day's shadow.

Under the ring of fire
a child remembers flashlight games—
rosy palm and fingers
against the light,
blood flowing in the webs.

Everything is distance and perspective,
cat and mouse, an apple's orbit
on a string above your mouth.

Tumbleweed

Somewhere out there, the dark
hugs itself until a bush
of it blossoms between
where you are, and where I sit
staring east out the window—
a tumbleweed of dark
gathering speed as it rolls
across the plains until
it stops at the foundation
of your house, looking innocent
in daylight, rather like
a rusting bale of chicken-wire
the wind plays like a harp
that knows by heart the notes
of your name.

A Bear Enters the Stream

A bear enters the stream
pawing for salmon, snags
wriggling flesh on its claws,

and the fog lifts,
sun storming the Earth
like an old woman's fits,
the incandescent whites of her eyes
rolling back and back
into the dark
while all her muscles twitch.

A bear enters the stream;
the salmon are running
home, the fog
leaves scales on our limbs
moist and shining.

For the Acequia Madre, Mother Ditch

Water flows again in the Acequia,
   snow-melt from the mountain
      gone dark in the dusk,
         its only light in moving.

Now above, now below,
   in and out of culverts,
      it bellies through cracked fields,

this dark old snake
   that takes my spirit
      into its swift mouth.

Vision Quest

The spider who lives
over the hole in the floor
in the corner of the teachers' bathroom
has a dim and dusty web.
I greet her silently
each time I turn toward her
to wash my hands.

I learn from her
how to wait, unmoving
attentive to what might
come up out of the dark.

Turtle Blessing

After the boy threw the pregnant turtle
hard against the brick wall
of the courtyard, screaming
"What are you, some kind of
fucking humanitarian?"
to the girl who called him crazy,
the creature bounced off,
crawled a few feet, blood
seeping into the weeds
from her cracked shell,
and stopped.

She died last night,
was buried, her eggs gone
with her into the earth.

This morning in the mist
by Seeley's Pond, an ancient turtle,
huge and black on the wet grass,
turns its blunt head this way, that,
as it crawls up the slope
toward the road, and I bless it
against the crunch of its dark shell,
against the driver who will not swerve.

Knife Song

As the knife approaches the light
it begins to sing, whining
like a saw blade, vibrating
to shed skin after skin
from its dull steel
until it is ready
for the marriage—
the slicing through a beam
so insubstantial
the knife knows
it has finally arrived
where cutting has no meaning
anymore, and the light
loves it anyway.

Living on a County Highway

Our yard is a shore of garbage.
All day it washes up
on the vapor trail of passing cars,
the stinking wind.
        Our trees,
tall weeds and thorn bush,
and peeling grape arbor behind the house
invite it.

Beer bottles, their smooth mouths
broken off, grind glass teeth,
dart like empty barracuda
across the sidewalk
and into the dirt hollows
where our grass used to be.

Styrofoam cups roll down the driveway.

Once, a plastic dropcloth
strewn like a torn mermaid
across the rose bushes
undulated all night in March moonlight.

And today, a large crumple of brown paper
presses itself tightly against the oak tree,
homing, trying to return to its source.

Dragonflies

At Yamadera Temple
a dragonfly lights on my finger.
"A blessing," says Kawasaki Tenko.

By the sacred pagoda on Mount Haguro
a dragonfly rests on the back of my hand
so long I become its swiveling head,
tissue wings,
and tiny, gripping feet.

And this morning on the car roof
we find a giant dragonfly,
a stranger here,
fallen from the sky in last night's storm,
or drowned and beaten down from some wet branch.

Carefully, I lift its tubular body,
stroke iridescent wings and crumpled legs,
willing it to quiver into life.

Tonight, wings brittle,
thorax hardened,
it sits on the dresser,
a permanent blessing,
and I enter the blue tunnel of its body,
passing its dessicated guts, withered heart,
until I reach its compound eyes
and see through them the sky
fracturing before me, flooded
with light.

Frogs in the Rice Paddies, Kawasaki

As we walk home in the humid night air,
on the raised macadam path
parting the farmer's rice paddy,
the frog song swells ahead of us,
gathers behind us;

but where we walk, silence
moves with us across the field,
like a cloud shadow passing
over the still waters
where a thousand frogs
chant all night.

Suddenly, I want to run
moving the music back and forth
under the hazy moon.
I want to leave the path,
fall down between green rows,
and sing.

Deer Crossing

This morning, the car in front of me
stops suddenly, waits
as five deer emerge from somebody's back yard,
crossing the frosty grass
to bound across the Boulevard
into the saplings of the Great Swamp.

I don't know what to do
about the pregnant doe
I counted dead by the side of the road
three mornings last week,
her white belly shining
in the sunrise;
about the young buck hit yesterday,
spun down midst broken glass,
weeping,
and police cars.

I only know the boundaries are blurring:
that buck whose antlers flowered on his head
like found money,
slept in your bed last night,
that doe in mine,
while we stumbled in our nakedness,
running on all fours
through thickets of dark trees
to freeze in the stunning light
of an unexpected clearing.

When I Saw the Wounded Pigeon

When I saw the wounded pigeon
struggling to rise from the roadway
below her roost in the girders
of the underpass, flapping
her good wing, not understanding
why her broken wing held
to the pavement, a useless weight;
when I felt the pain
in her right shoulder, looked up
with her at the others,
iridescent echoes above the dark
road's cold shadows, I cried
for her, driving up the hill
into the sun, my still obedient
foot on the accelerator.

The hill curved
until I could no longer see
her struggling, but all day
she has been trying to lift
that dead wing, all day
she has flapped and flapped
just beyond my reach.

In Deer Country

Part leaf, part shade,
they stand beside the road,
and we are foreign. Out there
at the edge of the clearing,
some drift into the sun,
faces lowered to crop clover,
backs flecked with light.

In deer country, they live
in their own time; even running,
their limbs flow softly into grass,
their bodies weave like water.
They are the old way
of moving on the Earth.

Like Mother

When she drove to work
through the woods of the reservation,
that hill of trees we have reserved
for all of us animals,
she saw the dead skunk
near the white line.
Another one dead on the road,
she thought and then forgot,

until at dusk,
coming around the same bend
into the gathering dark,
she met the skunk again
and saw beside it
two baby skunks pawing,
pawing, they just keep pawing
at the flattened scrap of fur
that still smells like mother.

The Only Cows Left in Piscataway

The only cows left in Piscataway
chew grass by the split-rail fence,
and fix their mild eyes on the horizon
where petroleum tanks squat.

The only cows left in Piscataway
breathe black smoke
settling on the pasture
like fog on a gray morning,
hang their heads over the fence
and fix mild eyes on trucks
spewing their way uphill.

The only cows left in Piscataway
eat grass in a field fertilized
by exhaust, and the farmer
wipes soot from their faces
before he milks them.

About Stone

Stone sings in the sun,
so low no one hears it but worms,
or the roots of tall trees.

Stone sings of the fire,
the original kiln,
and its long migration
to such peace

it suffers us.

How Can We Not

How can we not be lonely,
one species among the many,
having lost the mother tongue,
forgotten how to speak in the old way,
throats open, teeth shining
as the word slides over them,
growling, warbling, hissing
our breath?

Feather, fin, and fur
are no longer of our flesh
except for the dark fuzz in our armpits,
the springing hair of our heads,
the wiry tangle where we generate
others of ourselves.

How can we not be lonely?
Listen to the wind tonight,
how it teaches the trees
to know themselves;
how it carries the cries
of the neighbor's dog
to others of his kin;
how it wants us to join in.

For a Great Horned Owl

Tonight, like an early solstice,
the sky swings open,
the stars grow fierce,
and a chill wind rises in the sycamore,
keening among the dead and dying leaves
as it marries the cold to the dark.

Where I live, house after house
turns on its lights;
but on this wind, an owl
in a midnight pine forest
calls across twenty years
because I will not leave the tent
and walk barefoot through the trees
to find her.

Owl Dream

In my dream an owl
beats spread wings
against my window
promising a share
of her kill.

Small bones
lodge in my throat.
Blood and sinew
stain my tongue.

Her wings move faster now,
a white blizzard
against the glass.
Her eyes glare
over a harsh beak.

She wants my fingers,
little animals that squirm
on their own in the dark
of my sleep.

She wants to tell me
it's all right,
that we can both have
everything we need
from the same field.

This Morning's Birds

This morning's birds sail
above the drainage ditch,
black bodies rising
and falling as one,
as once they wheeled
from Brueghel's wooded hills
to hang in dark clouds
above the river.

These winter birds are foam
at the planet's edge,
waves of them pushing
against the sky, arcing up
and out until forced back
by air too thin, by gravity,
to the constant trees.
We are all their forest.

Light Years

The white birches flare
in the sunlight, mute
under the passing clouds,
rock toward one another,
pull apart.
Overhead, great clouds
drift slowly to
the rhythm of a breath
so distant there are years
between the breathing in
and breathing out
upon us all.

Driving Home

I can hear the trees today;
their bare branches trumpet
into the cloudy sky,
and beside the road
where the bulldozer has been,
the discord of raw stumps
discharges into the air.

Down the wooded slope,
yellow grasses sound
in the dusk, and two mallards
lift from the dark pond
into the rhythm of their wings,
rising so far above the earth,
I hear the rushing of their blood
as if it were the wind.

Just There

The way the trees beside this road
lift their branches into rain,
just there against the cloudy sky,
tells me they are glad to be
still blossoming, though they are old.

Last night in the sunset,
I saw the newborn leaves of one
light up like celery and give themselves
to a small wind, and I bowed my head
in that light.

Willow

The green window of the willow deep in the woods,
shining from among the still bare trees,
opens into the first sunlight
so pure its branches singe the air,
so bright that I remember living there.

Tulip

I watched its first green push
through bare dirt, where the builders
had dropped boards, shingles, plaster—
killing everything.
I could not recall what grew there,
what returned each spring,
but the leaves looked tulip,
and one morning it arrived,
a scarlet slash against the aluminum siding.

Mornings, on the way to my car,
I bow to the still bell
of its closed petals; evenings,
it greets me, light ringing
at the end of my driveway.

Sometimes I kneel
to stare into the yellow throat,
count the black tongues,
stroke the firm red mouth.
It opens and closes my days.
It has made me weak with love,
this god I didn't know I needed.

Dusk

I lower my ear
to the purple grass,
a murmuring that runs to the horizon
pearled with the dampness of dusk,
and all the shining sheep
like laughter scattered
here and there across a life
lie down where they are in the fields,
filling the dark spaces
between the spokes of some great wheel
before it creaks and rolls
into the sky.

The Way Home

There is a way home.
It runs through the cornfields beneath the stars,
rises like a river
to wash the apple trees below the barn.
If you are careful you will not disturb the snakes
who curl in the tall weeds
beside the grassy path your feet have known.

Sometimes in the distance
you will see the others,
silhouettes on moonlit hills
carrying hoes over their shoulders,
returning from their fields
even as you go to yours,
sure-footed as a goat
down the stubbled rows toward sleep.

When you climb to the graveyard on the hillside,
stop among the old ones,
take off your clothes,
lie down on the earth
with your head in the shadows
the moon throws between tombstones,
and begin to count the stars
in the Milky Way.

You will run out of numbers.
You will run out of words.
You will forget how to talk to the sky.
You will forget where you have come from,
or where you are going.
You will only know that you are light
among the stars,
that cornfields spiral out from you
on every side, shining corn
as far as you can see—
over the edge of the world,
that dark circle you have found
at last.

A Circle of Sheep

A circle of sheep in the twilight,
lying in the pale green grass,
their backs like ancient dolmens
bleaching under the darkening sky—

a circle of sheep
down at dusk
in a soft field,
sleeping.

Shadows surround them.
Their yellow eyes open
under the moon.

They rise, bleating,
to break from center,
white smudges, drifting
toward the dark horizon.

At the field's edge
cars rush by, headlights
probing the night.

After Bannock Point

We stood on the dirt road above the lake,
loose-limbed in the twilight like children,
the sunset held by the water
throwing a sheen on the tall, pale trunk
of the birch among dark pines.
Luminous along its whole left side,
its body lifted up, up, carrying
lake light back into the sky.
And I remembered the pale trunks
of our own bodies, naked
on that stony shore, felt them
stretching like the tree, tingling
with wind and sun against the dark.

In the Rain

In the rain, the earth shines;
leaves hold their sheen to the sky,
and I remember the weight of my hand
on your forehead, your taut skin
pale in the dark, my fingers curving
to fit your skull, the way water fits
everything it finds, its tributaries running
between black branches, green leaves
all the way to the ground.

For the Autumnal Equinox

How can I tell it,
this blue light that comes
at dusk, mottled
with cold gray clouds
blown down from the north?

Green leaves, already
curling on their stems,
cup it here and there—
a gleam off the lobe,
a flash from an underside
turned heavenward.

I think of the planes of a face—
cheekbones slanting,
forehead luminous;
or the flesh of any water
that gives itself completely
to the sky.

Waiting for the Train, Spring Lake, November

Waiting for the train
in sunlight too warm
for November, yesterday's rain
shining in blue puddles;
looking down the long vee
of the track, that steel finger
pointing somewhere else, always
somewhere else, its blue rail
humming in the unlikely heat,
is like standing on a platform
at the earth's edge, waiting
to swim into the clouds,
waiting to mount the blue
sky, carrying all the baggage
you'll ever need.

The Winter Fields

Sunlight in the cattails
over the dark river,
spills into pampas grass
that bends in waves of winter light
from a sun so much nearer to us now
these fields seem on fire.

I drive the road between them,
left cheek rosy,
left ear burning in the lens
of the closed window.

Three hunters in red jackets,
their hats like roadside flares,
move along a line of distant trees,
stalking others like the deer who lies
beside the road, her body incandescent
with mud and dried blood,

and I know I am alive this afternoon,
my face flaming against the blue sky.

February Storm

Somewhere up the hill a neighbor's dog barks.
Snow swims through us shepherding the cold
while above the clouds the full moon turns
a dark face toward the stars.

Shadows shift under the juniper.
Sparrows sleep near the twisted trunk.
Curled against your back I lie with you
in a warm bed, our down quilt of white
feathers plucked from frozen geese,
blood gone black on the ice.

The moon sets red over the Earth's rim.
Drifts slope from all our doors,
and the wind in the corners of our room
wants us now.

Reading the Tea Leaves

After winter rain
dead leaves have steeped
in the gutter.

Easter eggs dipped in this tea
would darken
to barnyard brown.

On the neighbor's lawn an inflated swan
adrift on a stake like a weather vane
wheels slowly to face us.

I bend over the puddle,
stir with one finger
the cold silt at bottom,

watching the shredded leaves rise,
swirl and settle, as if I were
shaking them in a tiny globe.

Night Watch

All night I watch for
the movement of snow
toward water.

Waking again and again,
I check the window
looking for a thaw
under the streetlight,
a white withdrawal
at the edge of the lawn.

Across the planet, missiles
discover one another,
kin embracing kin
in the night sky.

How briefly each one lives
above or in the dirt
that cannot refuse it.

Two Ravens

Two ravens circle above the snow,
blacker than before.
Some dead thing is down there in the wasteland
where last summer, a few pieces of cardboard,
an old rug, and the ashes of a camp fire
told of someone's home.

This morning, snow fills the tin can
that glowed like a star each time
the hot butt of a cigarette found
its dark mouth;
and snow enters the cardboard house
spread like a picnic cloth
beneath the juniper in the arroyo.

Even the pack of wild dogs
whose footprints stain the frosts of autumn,
whose dark barking helps the sun rise,
is lost in this snow, this radiant snow
whiter than before because two ravens
bless it with black wings.

Whale Song

Whalebones arc among white stones.
Bleached old guardians, the great ribs close
like igloos on each grave.

Driven into dirt the bones are still.
One thinks of Jonah and the bellied black,
the hard enfolding.

Sun bounces round the ribs that rim the whole—
They move! They move again, a single ripple,
lean as a xylophone.

The souls of these whales long ago returned
to the cold seas, the gray sky—
and now this rhythm,
this dance in a white space?

The Weather of the Sun

The weather of the sun
dissolves the mist that rises
from your body like yeast—
mist caught so long
in a web of trees
it has married them,
pressed its wet mouth
to each leaf—each vein
sucking sap.

You have forgotten
the sun, how it paints
your limbs gold, how it brings
lemons to life in a wooden bowl,
how it buzzes with fruit flies
in the orchard.

Your sweat is a tribute.

Asleep You Are a River

Asleep, you are a river
    face rippling over stones
        legs drifting like branches
            torso heaving currents.

When you stretch your arms upward
    you call tributaries home,
        breed clouds from your fingertips.

Even your breathing
    is a long journey
        to the sea.

Sister Death

My death grazes just out of sight
over my right shoulder.
I hear the whisper of green
between her lips.
I imagine her as mare
heavy with foal,
tail swishing flies from her strong back,
eyes brown as a farm pond.

Each day I toss a lump of sugar
back into that unseen pasture,
murmur soothing words under my breath.

Wherever I go she migrates with me.
Even in winter
when fodder is scarce,
I feel her warm breath on my neck
and dream of bundled hay in a heated stall.

One day in some field
neither of us has visited
I will forget to toss the sugar
or to dream of hay,
and my death will canter closer
whinnying softly
until her nose finds my palm.

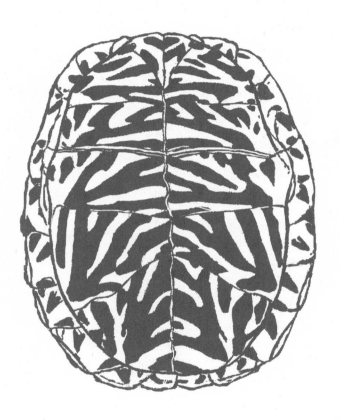

Set in Monotype Bembo
with titling in Blado italic,
Griffo's punch &
a scribe's hand,
wings
for
ink.

book design by J. Bryan

Penny Harter lives in Santa Fe, New Mexico. Much of her current work reflects ecological concerns and an imperative sensibility toward co-habitation with other species. She has won fellowships and awards from the New Jersey State Council on the Arts, the Geraldine R. Dodge Foundation, and the Poetry Society of America. Her previous books include: *STAGES and VIEWS* (Katydid Books); *GRANDMOTHER'S MILK* (Singular Speech Press), and *SHADOW PLAY: NIGHT HAIKU* (Simon & Schuster Books for Young Readers).

Bari Long is artist-in-residence at the Randall Davey Audubon Center at the end of Canyon Road in Santa Fe.